THE DEPARTMENT OF EDUCATION

A LOOK BEHIND THE SCENES

By Amy Rechner

Content Consultant:
David E. Kirkland, PhD, JD
Associate Professor, English and Urban Education
New York University

Compass Point Books are published by Capstone
1710 Roe Crest Drive, North Mankato, Minnesota 56003
www.mycapstone.com

Library of Congress Cataloging-in-Publication Data
Names: Rechner, Amy, author.
Title: The Department of Education : a look behind the scenes / by Amy Rechner.
Description: North Mankato, Minnesota : Compass Point Books, 2019. |
Series: U.S. government behind the scenes | Includes bibliographical references and index. |
Audience: Age 12-17.
Identifiers: LCCN 2018043270| ISBN 9780756559021 (hardcover) | ISBN 9780756559113 (pbk.)
Subjects: LCSH: United States. Department of Education—Juvenile literature. | Education and state—United States—Juvenile literature. | Federal aid to education—United States—Juvenile literature.
Classification: LCC LB2807 .R43 2019 | DDC 379.73—dc23
LC record available at https://lccn.loc.gov/2018043270

Editorial Credits:
Amy Kortuem, editor; Terri Poburka, designer; Jo Miller, media researcher; Tori Abraham, production specialist

Image Credits:
AP Images, 21; Getty Images: Bettmann/Contributor, 13, 14, Cynthia Johnson/Contributor, 24, Justin Sullivan/Staff, 54, Spencer Grant/Contributor, 16; iStockphoto: baona, Cover; Newscom: Everett Collection, 49, MCT/Heather Stone, 39, Reuters/Jason Reed, 27, UPI, 33, UPI/NASA, 7, UPI/Pete Marovich, 29, ZUMA Press/TASS, 6; Shutterstock: GaudiLab, 57, HunterMatthew, 45, 52, James Kirkikis, 47, Monkey Business Images, 42, Rawpixel.com, 5, YanLev, 30, zimmytws, 37; Wikimedia: U.S. Dept. of Education, 35, 50, White House, 10, 19 (all), Yoichi Okamoto, 15

Design Elements:
Shutterstock: anndypit, ben Bryant, RetroClipArt, Tobias Steinert

Printed and bound in the USA.
PA49

TABLE OF CONTENTS

CHAPTER ONE

It *Was* Rocket Science

"Wow, you're good at math. Ever thought about engineering?"

"Would you like to go to science camp this summer?"

"Those girls built a robot that can pick up dog poop!"

For the last two decades, students have been urged to explore STEM classes or activities. STEM is short for science, technology, engineering, and math. Because of a shortage of qualified professionals in those fields, the Department of Education under Presidents George W. Bush and Barack Obama created a big push to educate future experts. While the push was a success, the market for STEM professionals is growing faster than students can earn their degrees.

The first time this happened there was no Department of Education. For that matter, there was no STEM. The Department of Education as it is today was created in 1979. The term STEM was first used in 2001. But the story of STEM and the Department of Education starts in 1957 with a bleeping sound in the key of A-flat. The sound came from a Russian satellite that circled the globe. Military and short-wave radio operators tracked its progress as an alarmed nation waited to see what would happen next.

The space race spurred U.S. interest in science, technology, engineering, and math (STEM) education.

The Soviet-Russian space program's launch of *Sputnik* was the first satellite ever put into orbit. It was during the Cold War, the time after World War II. The United States and the Soviet Union were competing with each other for world dominance. Since no one wanted to use nuclear weapons again, they had what was called a "cold war," using threats rather than aggression. The United States was certain that its military and space technology were superior, so *Sputnik* caused a panic across the United States. People were afraid that if the Soviets could launch a satellite, they could also launch missiles to bomb the United States.

The Soviets were the first to orbit Earth with their satellite, Sputnik.

While the Army Security Agency, the U.S. Army's electronic intelligence branch, monitored *Sputnik*'s course around Earth, the government scrambled to act. The United States was not only behind in the space race, but it didn't have enough scientists and engineers to catch up. Congress had not appropriated any funding for education in three years. Education was mostly paid for by state and local taxes.

Senator Lister Hill of Alabama changed the name of the education funding bill to the National Defense Education Act. By tying education funding to an increase in national security, Congress passed the bill and President Dwight D. Eisenhower approved it in 1958. The National Defense Education Act gave loans and grants to college students and teachers in science, math, and technology education.

Additional funds were used to expand college library collections in those subjects. Library funding was also later extended to elementary and high schools.

The realization that the United States wasn't ahead in the space race or in education was a jolt for Congress, the president, and the nation as a whole. The government resolved to catch up and surpass the Soviet Union. The National Aeronautics and Space Administration (NASA) was created in July 1958. Congress got the United States into orbit.

But there wouldn't be a Department of Education for another 21 years.

President Dwight D. Eisenhower (center) commissioned two scientists to lead the newly formed NASA in 1958.

The Smallest Seat at the Table

The Department of Education is the smallest department represented in the cabinet. The cabinet is a group of advisors to the president. They each represent a department in the executive branch of the government. The cabinet meets frequently to advise the president on matters related to their departments. Cabinet members are called secretaries. They are in charge of areas including Defense, Commerce, Treasury, Energy, Labor, and Homeland Security. The vice president is also a cabinet member.

Each president appoints secretaries for each department. They replace those appointed by the previous president. The Senate must approve the president's choice before the secretary can begin his or her job. The Senate does not always approve presidential appointees. Sometimes the candidate is unqualified or has a conflict of interest. The Senate needs a majority vote to approve a candidate. If there is a tie, the vice president, who is also president of the Senate, casts the tie-breaking vote. If a candidate isn't confirmed by the Senate, the president needs to find someone else.

The Department of Education employs a staff of about 4,400. That is about 4 percent the size of the Department of Justice staff, which at last count numbered more than 107,000. The department's annual budget depends on what the president requests from Congress each year.

Operating Structure of the Department of Education

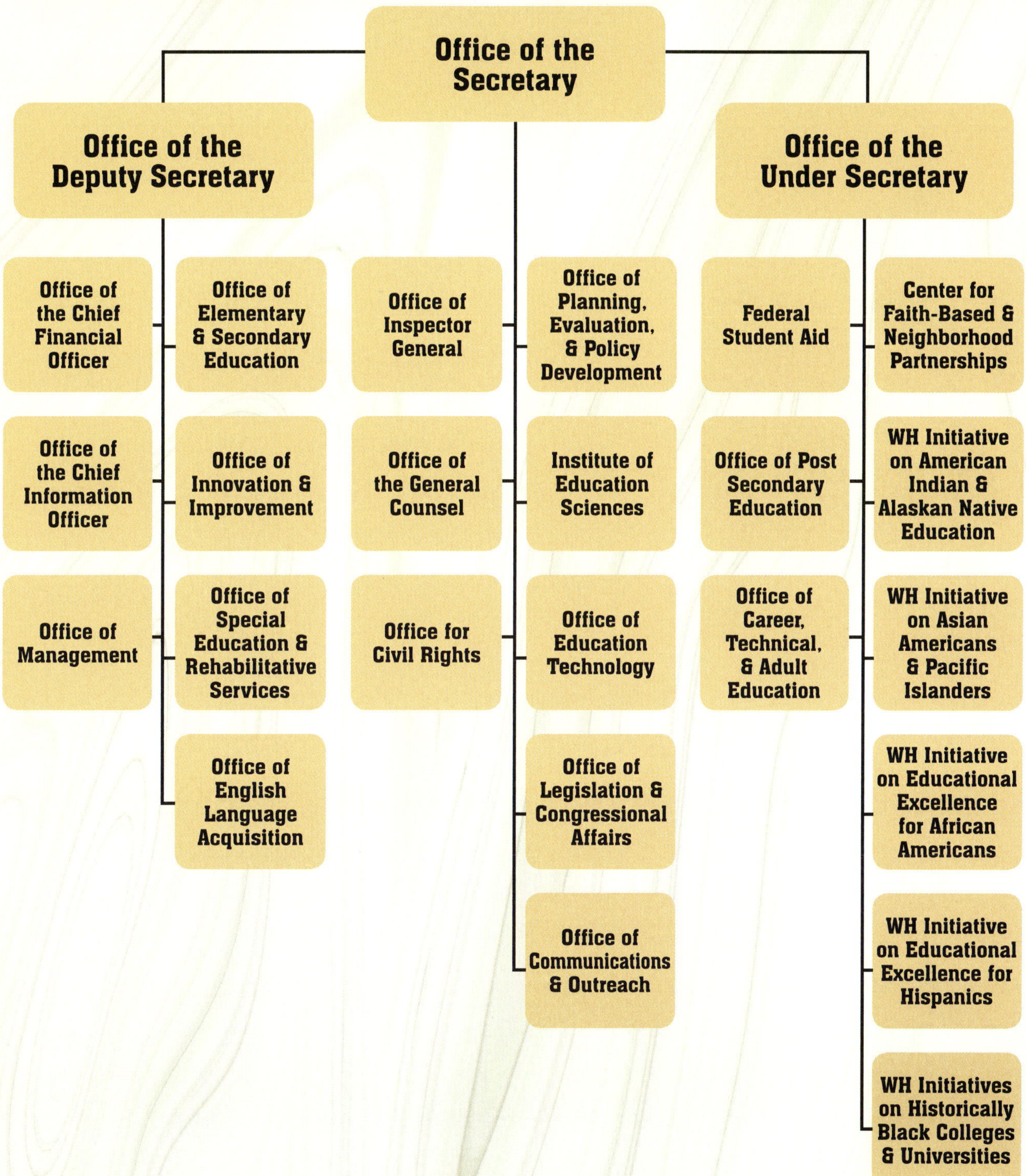

President Ronald Reagan disagreed with the need for a Department of Education.

Not all presidents have agreed that education should be a federal issue. For instance, President Ronald Reagan tried to eliminate the Department of Education completely from his 1983 budget. He wanted to put the money into defense. Throughout Reagan's presidency Congress gave the Department of Education a larger budget than the president had asked for. In contrast, Congress regularly approved less money than President Bill Clinton requested for education during his administration.

Although some presidents preferred to leave education to the states, U.S. voters have made it clear that it is an important policy issue. Each president's legacy is affected by the action—or inaction—of the administration on education issues. Halfway through his presidency, Reagan switched his position on education to one that was more popular with voters.

The Department of Education has been a political ping-pong ball since the beginning. Republicans hold one ping-pong paddle and Democrats hold the other. The Republican Party believes that education is a state issue and the federal government should stay out of it. Democrats want federal support for education. They worry that without government help many educational programs and scholarships will end. The opposing sides have batted this issue back and forth for more than 150 years.

With each new president, there is a new plan for education. More than one president has planned to abolish the Department of Education completely.

How much does your state spend on your public school education?

Alabama	$9,236
Alaska	$17,510
Arizona	$7,613
Arkansas	$9,846
California	$11,495
Colorado	$9,575
Connecticut	$18,958
Delaware	$14,713
District of Columbia	$19,159
Florida	$8,920
Georgia	$9,769
Hawaii	$13,748
Idaho	$7,157
Illinois	$14,180
Indiana	$9,856
Iowa	$11,150
Kansas	$9,960
Kentucky	$9,863
Louisiana	$11,038
Maine	$13,278
Maryland	$14,206
Massachusetts	$15,593
Michigan	$11,668
Minnesota	$12,382
Mississippi	$8,702
Missouri	$10,313
Montana	$11,348
Nebraska	$12,299
Nevada	$8,960
New Hampshire	$15,340
New Jersey	$18,402
New Mexico	$9,693
New York	$22,366
North Carolina	$8,792
North Dakota	$13,373
Ohio	$12,102
Oklahoma	$8,097
Oregon	$10,842
Pennsylvania	$15,418
Rhode Island	$15,532
South Carolina	$10,249
South Dakota	$9,176
Tennessee	$8,810
Texas	$9,016
Utah	$6,953
Vermont	$17,873
Virginia	$11,432
Washington	$11,534
West Virginia	$11,291
Wisconsin	$11,456
Wyoming	$16,442

Source: 2016 Annual Survey of School System Finances, U.S. Census Bureau

CHAPTER TWO

From Beta to 4.0: Versions of the Education Department

The first president to shine a spotlight on education was the 17th president, Andrew Johnson. He created the first Department of Education in 1867, staffed with four employees. The stated goal of Johnson's Department of Education was to collect data on education and teaching and to share the information to aid in the creation of effective school districts. Before that, centralized schools were still rare. Many children were taught at home. Much of the nation was too rural for school districts to be practical, since farming seasons and distance made regular schooling difficult.

Even at the beginning, people were worried about federal interference in schools. Many Congressmen felt the Department's mission was too intrusive, and moved to shut it down. In 1868, after the Department's first report to Congress, it was demoted to an Office of Education and absorbed by the Department of the Interior.

George McLaurin (left) was the first black student admitted to the University of Oklahoma (1948). He was required to sit away from white students.

After that, the federal government mostly left education to the states until 1953. At that time, Dwight D. Eisenhower created the Department of Health, Education, and Welfare to serve the rapidly growing population. By the end of his presidency the education department he created had provided funding for thousands of new schools. It had expanded library services to more than 30 million rural citizens.

Eisenhower's administration also upheld civil rights laws for black students. The fight for equality in education began with an 1896 Supreme Court case called *Plessy v. Ferguson*. At that time many areas of the United States, especially the South, were completely segregated. White and black students did not attend the same schools. Black students had to go to school in rundown buildings with outdated books. In *Plessy v. Ferguson,* the Court ruled that segregation was legal so long as the school facilities were separate but equal. However, that law was never enforced, and school quality was unequal in many ways.

Black students who had previously been barred from Little Rock Central High School were escorted in by federal troops.

In 1954 another Supreme Court ruling, *Brown v. Board of Education*, overturned *Plessy*. The Court ruled that racial segregation in schools was unconstitutional. Black students in the South bravely enrolled in whites-only schools in pursuit of a better education. When nine black high school students tried to enter Little Rock Central High School in 1957, they were blocked by an angry, threatening mob. The mob was protected by the Arkansas National Guard. Governor Orval Faubus refused to obey the law and wouldn't let the students in. President Eisenhower had to send in federal troops to escort the nine students through the crowd into the high school.

Brown v. Board of Education didn't solve segregation. Many school districts, including Little Rock, Arkansas, closed public schools instead of allowing black students to attend. White students in Prince Edward County, Virginia, received tuition vouchers to attend segregated private schools instead. It wasn't until Lyndon B. Johnson was elected president in 1964 that education for all became a federal priority. Johnson unveiled a series of programs called the Great Society that were meant to eliminate poverty and racial injustice. His reforms included creating federal housing programs, creating Medicare, and raising the minimum wage. He signed the Civil Rights Act of 1964, which bars all schools and universities that receive federal funds from discriminating against students based on their race or national origin.

Johnson, a former high school and college teacher of government and debate, also got down to the business of education in his presidency. In 1965 he signed the Elementary and Secondary Education Act (ESEA). It provided federal grant money to states and K-12 school districts. ESEA outlined most of the funding that the Department of Education now controls. Title I is the main part of the law. It provides funding to schools and districts with low-income families.

President Lyndon B. Johnson signed the ESEA Act in 1965, which still provides funding to schools.

Federal courts mandated busing to achieve racial balance in Boston schools in 1974.

President Johnson's original ESEA provided funding for low-income schools and districts, school libraries, and preschools. Before he left office in 1969 he created the Bilingual Education Act, which supported programs for students learning English, and the Handicapped Children's Early Education Assistance Act, which funded preschool and early childhood programs for children with special needs.

In 1965 Johnson also signed the Higher Education Act (HEA) into law. It offered funding to colleges and universities. It also made financial aid available to students for college tuition in the form of loans, grants, work-study programs, and scholarships.

The Elementary and Secondary Education Act continued to expand under President Richard Nixon. He signed into law many important additions, including more funding for students with disabilities and for refugee and low-income children. He also authorized an official definition of "gifted and talented." His most significant contribution was in 1972 when he signed Title IX into law. Title IX prohibits discrimination or harassment based on sex in any organization or institution that receives federal funding. That was the final addition made to the original ESEA.

In the early 1970s, education became a hot campaign issue. It reflected the racial turmoil in the nation. Local school districts were still fighting desegregation. One of the strategies to mix student populations was forced integration through busing. This happened mainly in large cities such as Boston, Massachusetts; Detroit, Michigan; Louisville, Kentucky; and Washington, D.C. Students from mostly black schools were sent by bus to mostly white schools to create a more diverse student body.

Elementary and Secondary Education Act of 1965 (ESEA)

Title I

Funding to schools and districts with low-income families

Title II

Funding for school libraries, textbooks, preschool programs (1969 amendment provided funding for programs for refugee children and children in public housing)

Title III

Funding for support services and education centers to offer educational opportunities for summer or non-school days; funding for special education in rural areas
(1968 amendment provided the basis for The Bilingual Education Act and the Education of the Handicapped Act)

Title IV

Funding for research and training

Title V

Supplementary grants to state departments

Title VI

General provisions of the law (1969 amendment dedicated funds to the education of individuals with disabilities)

Title VII (1969)

Bolstered the Vocational Educational Act of 1963 (1984 amendment provided assistance for bilingual services)

Title VIII (1969)

Provided definition of gifted and talented; established Teacher Corps

Title IX (1972)

Prohibited discrimination based on sex at any school or program receiving federal funds

Many school districts resisted busing, so students stayed in their home districts. In 1971 the Supreme Court ruled in *Swann v. Charlotte-Mecklenburg Board of Education* that the school district had to integrate its schools using busing. Until that ruling, the school district was using busing to segregate the schools. Like many other districts in the South, they bused white students to white schools beyond walking distance. In spite of the Supreme Court ruling, neither Nixon nor the next president, Gerald Ford, liked the idea of forced desegregation. They felt the real solution was to focus on improving the schools rather than fixing the racial imbalance. Both ruled in favor of busing black children into white neighborhoods, with reservations. Nixon publicly expressed his disapproval of it but stated that as president he understood his responsibility to carry out the Court's wishes. Busing was used in cities with large black populations until the 1990s, and still continues today in Louisville, Kentucky.

The Changing Involvement of Government in Education Under Three Presidents

Department (Office) of Education
1867–1868
Andrew Johnson
(1865–1869)

Department of Health, Education, and Welfare
1953–1979
Dwight D. Eisenhower
(1953–1961)

Department of Education
Established 1979
Jimmy Carter
(1977–1981)

In 1979 President Jimmy Carter split the Department of Health, Education, and Welfare into two new departments. The health and welfare parts became the Department of Health and Human Services.

Carter wanted a Department of Education so the issue of education could draw increased federal attention. He also wanted to create a system at the federal level to support the state and local institutions. By creating one department focused solely on education, he hoped to cut down on red tape and paperwork at the local and state level. He also predicted that by eliminating layers of bureaucracy at the state and federal level, fewer staff would be needed, and taxes used to pay salaries would go down.

The next president, Ronald Reagan, called it "President Carter's new bureaucratic boondoggle." He vowed to get rid of it completely. He didn't think it was necessary and planned to split up its responsibilities among other departments. However, his first years in office were busy with the economy and international affairs. Reagan appointed Terrel Bell as education secretary, and told him to dismantle the department. Reagan paid little attention to it during the rest of his first term.

Instead, Bell put together a study of how American schools were doing. The 1983 report looked at student scores in reading and math across grades, schools, and sub-groups. The sub-groups detailed scores among English learners, low-income students, minority students, and so forth.

It took 18 months to collect all the information. The results were not encouraging. Called "A Nation at Risk," the report warned of sliding scores and lower student performance in U.S. schools. The experts who wrote the report made recommendations on how to improve student and school performance.

- 4 years of high school English
- 3 years each of high school math, science, and social studies
- Foreign language study beginning in grade school

- Expanded school years and school days
- Closer oversight of teacher performance and competence
- Raised admission standards at four-year colleges
- Raised standardized test achievement standards from one schooling level to the next

After the report was turned in, Reagan held a ceremony at the White House. Copies of the report were handed out to the media. Reagan thanked the report's writers for supporting his plans to encourage school prayer, increase tuition tax credits, and abolish the Department of Education. The next day newspapers ran front-page stories about the report. Although they noticed that it did not include Reagan's plans, the papers were full of praise for the direction the administration

President Ronald Reagan (center) appointed Terrel Bell (left) secretary of education.

was appearing to take. Reagan probably should have read the report before the White House ceremony because none of his pet plans were even mentioned in it. In addition to the recommended changes to schools and curriculum, the report noted that the federal government played an essential role in helping key groups of students. It said it must remain involved to ensure compliance with "constitutional and civil rights" and to "provide student financial assistance and research and graduate training." Reagan disliked the report once he read it but by then it was too late to reject it. Public reaction was so positive that he decided to go with it, since he wanted to be reelected in 1984. That was the end of his administration's attempts to close the Department of Education. A 2011 article in *The Washington Post* asked education scholars who they considered the best "education president." Ronald Reagan was mentioned more than once because of his support of the "A Nation at Risk" recommendations.

"The Bedrock of Democracy"

Arguments about school reform, standards, and federal involvement continued through the rest of the 20th century. Reagan's successor in office, President George H.W. Bush, a Republican, declared himself the "education president." Bush wanted to create national standardized tests to increase student and school performance. He gathered together governors from all the states in a meeting to discuss national goals for education. He created an education plan called America 2000, with stronger standards in several subjects.

Bush added funds to the Department of Education's budget to draft a national education curriculum. His plan did not pass Congress. The proposed America 2000 Excellence in Education Act was blocked in both the House and Senate by Republican-controlled education committees. The bill was Bush's idea, and 67 House Republicans and 20 Senate Republicans sponsored it, but it was never debated or voted upon. Republicans controlled both the House and the Senate.

Their party platform states that the federal government should not be involved in education.

Bush did succeed in signing the Americans with Disabilities Act into law in 1990. This civil rights act prohibits discrimination against people with disabilities in any public or private institution that receives federal funding. All colleges, universities, community colleges, and trade schools must provide equal access and accommodations for students with disabilities. All programs, including extracurricular activities, must be made accessible according to the law.

That same year Bush signed the Individuals with Disabilities Education Act (IDEA). It oversees how states and agencies help babies, children, and young adults with disabilities. It expanded President Ford's Early Education of the Handicapped Act to cover younger children. Greater technology, more and better-trained special education teachers, and better student outcomes are some of the goals that the Education Department's Office for Special Education Programs (OSEP) strives for. IDEA also absorbed part of Nixon's Rehabilitation Act of 1973, which helps people with disabilities overcome barriers to employment. Working with state training centers, the Rehabilitation Services Administration (RSA) opened technical assistance centers to offer further help to people with disabilities who wish to work.

Even though President George H.W. Bush was a Republican and Bill Clinton was a Democrat, they held similar views about education reform. As governor of Arkansas, Clinton was an enthusiastic participant in Bush's meeting on education standards. When he was running for president, Clinton called public schools the "bedrock of democracy." He spoke strongly about investing in the future of the U.S. through education.

Clinton's Goals 2000 program was in many ways an expansion of Bush's America 2000 program. His Improving America's Schools Act of 1994 added amendments to the Elementary and Secondary Education Act. The amendments defined clear assessment standards in education; expanded loans and grants for low-income students; and supported control of education by the states. Many of

Presidents Bill Clinton (left) and George H.W. Bush were both strong advocates of the Department of Education.

his changes affected Title I of ESEA by offering further guarantees to low-income, refugee, and other at-risk children. They would no longer be separated from the rest of the student body, as they had been for years. In addition, school districts receiving Title I funds were required to identify low-performing schools and take steps to improve them.

When drafting America 2000, President Bush had requested history education standards designed by educators. The submitted plan was very different from the traditional narrative that excluded minorities and any information that showed the United States in a bad light. It was submitted to Congress in 1994, two years after President Bush left office. Congress, still controlled by Republicans, rejected the proposal by a vote of 99 to 1, stating that the government should stay out of education.

In 1995, with the federal government pulling back, governors and heads of business took on the challenge of national curriculum standards. Corporate executives pledged support in their states as standards were developed at state and local levels. They promised to take the existence of school standards into account when choosing where to open new businesses. In addition, business interest groups were created to help states set academic standards for all students. The U.S. government would not take up the question of standards for another five years when another president was in office.

Secrets of Presidential Education

Abraham Lincoln had less than one year of schooling. Most of his early education came from reading books borrowed from neighbors. He took notes on boards when there was no writing paper.

Andrew Johnson never went to school. He had people read to him until his wife taught him to read and write.

Theodore Roosevelt was educated at home by tutors while he battled severe asthma. After he built up his strength he attended Harvard University.

William McKinley attended college for a year, then became a country schoolteacher. When the Civil War broke out, he enlisted in the Union army.

Dwight Eisenhower had learning difficulties that were later thought to be a form of dyslexia.

Lyndon Johnson taught government in school before going into government.

Jimmy Carter was the first person from his father's side of the family to graduate high school. He studied engineering in college before going to the U.S. Naval Academy at Annapolis.

Bill Clinton worked as a clerk for the Senate Foreign Relations Committee while attending Georgetown University in Washington, D.C. He won a Rhodes scholarship to Oxford University in England and then went on to Yale Law School.

Barack Obama attended grade school in Indonesia and Hawaii, high school in Hawaii, and college in Los Angeles and New York. After Harvard Law School, he worked as a law professor at the University of Chicago.

CHAPTER THREE

New Century, New Approach

By the year 2000, 17 years after "A Nation at Risk" was published in 1983, test scores in U.S. schools had not improved much. Despite increased funding and efforts at improvement, the nation's schools still ranked well below those in many other countries. Thirty-two countries were ranked in an international comparison. The U.S. was 15th in reading, 18th in math, and 14th in science. When President George W. Bush took office in 2001, he was eager to take on the challenge of improving the nation's scores.

Bush called himself the "educator in chief." His education reform plan was called No Child Left Behind (NCLB). This ambitious new plan updated and replaced Goals 2000/ESEA. It changed the way the Department of Education and the nation's schools worked.

President George W. Bush signed the No Child Left Behind Act into law in 2002.

Under Title I of Goals 2000/ESEA, the Department of Education distributed more than $14 billion each year through funding and grant programs. No Child Left Behind complicated the distribution formula. It tied school funding to school performance. Beginning in 2002 the amount of funding a school might receive depended on its teacher quality and standardized test results in math and reading. The idea was to improve schools serving low-income, minority, special needs, and English-learning students.

The pressure to produce high test scores had a major effect on schools and students. In many cases classroom time was taken up with studies related to the standardized tests. Other subjects such as social studies or science were neglected. Teachers felt they had no choice but to focus on the test subjects, which were typically math and language arts. If their students didn't do well and test scores were low, the teacher would be blamed and sometimes even fired.

Under NCLB the states set achievement targets and issued report cards of school performance. Sometimes low-performing schools had their staffs completely replaced or were closed down altogether. The states reported results to the Department of Education.

By the time NCLB was up for renewal in 2007 it was clear that it needed a lot of work. Test scores had not really changed among the disadvantaged students the program was intended to help. The increased testing and reporting was drowning schools, states, and the Department of Education in paperwork.

One Education Law, Three Names

Elementary & Secondary Education Act 1965	No Child Left Behind Act 2002	Every Student Succeeds Act 2015

Congress reviews the elementary and secondary education law for approval every five years.

President Barack Obama signed the Every Student Succeeds Act into law in 2015.

When President Barack Obama took office, he knew he would have to address the problems created by No Child Left Behind. He would also have to find a way to improve schools and student scores. In 2009 President Obama introduced Race to the Top, a three-year competition from 2010 to 2012 between states for federal funds. States were challenged to accomplish three tasks:

- Turn around low-achieving schools
- Encourage the opening of charter schools, which are privately run public schools established by an agreement (charter) between a state school board and an outside group
- Improve teacher and principal effectiveness

Students taking the first computer-based assessments on Common Core standards struggled with technical issues.

Race to the Top achieved its goal of getting many state governments to discuss or initiate education policy changes. It also led most of the nation's governors and state school officers to collaborate on new standards. They created the Common Core State Standards. Obama's Department of Education approved them. States were urged to adopt the Common Core standards so the nation would share national, competitive standards in education. States were not required to use Common Core standards but those that did were awarded federal funds. All states were asked to set higher standards of achievement for their students.

The Common Core standards were introduced in schools in the 2013–2014 school year. For many in the education community it was a difficult transition. The new standards were higher than many existing standards. Students spent a stressful year catching up to the new level for their grade.

A greater issue was the quality of the assessment testing. The two companies that provided the official tests to the school districts rushed the process of creating them. The tests were also rolled out in the 2013–2014 school year. That created big problems for teachers and students. Teachers had little preparation time or training in the new curriculum that students were going to be tested on. The computer-based assessments used technology schools weren't familiar with or that failed during test-taking. Further, an increased amount of time was set aside for testing, despite the objections of many parents and teachers. Students reported computer failures during a test one day, followed by a 15-minute test in a 45-minute block of time the next day, with no way to occupy the extra time.

By 2014 the Common Core curriculum standards had been put into use and accepted. However, many states abandoned the official tests within two years of its implementation. Most chose to write their own assessment tests. They mixed some questions from the official tests with content provided by a teachers' committee appointed by the state.

As the Race to the Top competition drew to a close, President Obama was ready to introduce his replacement for No Child Left Behind. In 2015 he introduced the Every Student Succeeds Act (ESSA). That became the name of the education law. It gives states more control over education funding and achievements. Its stated mission is "quality education for all students in all public schools."

As part of Every Student Succeeds, each state sets its own goals and achievement standards. The state submits its plan each year to the Department of Education for approval. Once the department gives the OK, the state passes on the new standards and recommendations to the schools. Schools and teachers collaborate on choosing curriculum and classroom materials that meet the standards.

When teachers plan their school year, they need to balance test time and standards with the rest of the material students need to learn. The teachers figure out their lesson plans, classroom activities, and tests for the year. The state gives standardized tests to see how much students have improved. The results are sent back to the Department of Education. The department tracks the testing results and state performance.

One of Donald Trump's presidential campaign promises was to abolish the Department of Education. He felt strongly that education was a local issue and that the federal government should stay out of it. The Department of Education under President Trump has not yet addressed issues of curriculum or school performance.

In 2017 President Donald Trump signed a resolution overturning parts of President Obama's Every Student Succeeds Act.

CHAPTER FOUR

Responsibilities of the Education Department

About 4,400 people work at the Department of Education. The department supports the president's education plan, manages data and statistics, enforces federal education laws, and provides information resources for teachers, parents, and students. Most important, it supervises the distribution of federal education funding.

Although the position of education secretary and one or two others are appointed by the president, most of the workers at the department are administrators who have worked in the department for a long time. They are devoted to keeping the work of the department moving even as education plans change at the top level. The workers come from many different backgrounds. Some come from the world of finance, many are lawyers, and many started as educators. Some spend their entire careers at the Department of Education.

When a president wants to start a new program, such as President Bush's No Child Left Behind, the appointed education secretary and staff provide support. Staff work with the White House to write the bill and help craft legislation with members of Congress. When Bush was promoting No Child Left Behind, Secretary Margaret Spellings traveled across the country and held public meetings to explain the program to parents and teachers.

Under the secretary's direction, the Department's Office of Communications Outreach sends out the president's education message through news announcements, speeches, photos, newsletters, blogs, and even social media. It also writes a lot of the content for the department's website.

President George W. Bush appointed Margaret Spellings secretary of education in 2005.

The National Center for Education Statistics is an office within the Department of Education. Mountains of data are collected, analyzed, and turned into reports. About 110 employees wade through statistics about student performance across the nation; international comparisons of student performance; studies on early childhood development; and library use. Each state submits information about how their schools did on assessments. The department also examines how national and local education money is spent. The reports they write about spending at schools, the cost of college, and the general condition of American education are given to Congress.

Were all secretaries of education teachers?

No! Look at the range of experience our Education secretaries have brought to the department.

President	Secretary	K-12 Teacher?
Jimmy Carter	Shirley Hufstedler	No
Ronald Reagan	Terrel H. Bell	Yes
Ronald Reagan	William J. Bennett	No
George H.W. Bush	Lauro F. Cavazos	No
George H.W. Bush	Ted Sanders	Yes
George H.W. Bush	Lamar Alexander	No
Bill Clinton	Richard Riley	No
George W. Bush	Roderick Paige	Yes
George W. Bush	Margaret Spellings	No
Barack Obama	Arne Duncan	No
Barack Obama	John B. King Jr.	Yes
Donald Trump	Betsy DeVos	No

Money Managers

One third of the Department of Education staff works in the federal Student Aid department. This is the department that oversees student loans, grants, and other types of aid to pay for college. They process all of the applications for grants and loans from students. They issue the checks to those who are approved for them. When loans are being repaid, the staff works to make sure the process goes smoothly.

In the Higher Education Act, Title IV made financial aid available for college in the form of loans, grants, work-study programs, and scholarships. High school students with an eye on college or trade school fill out a giant form called the Free Application for Federal Student Aid (FAFSA). The FAFSA form is a student's entry into the world of financial aid. Each year about 20 million high school students submit a FAFSA when planning for college.

One task of the department is to make loans and other funding more accessible to students seeking higher education.

Once the FAFSA is on file, the Department of Education can help a student figure out what kind of financial aid to apply for. It has resources to help students look for scholarships from government and colleges as well as outside sources. Many scholarships are given by private companies or municipal organizations.

The Department of Education also sponsors some federal grants for students. Like scholarships, grants are gifts of money that do not have to be repaid. Students must apply for the grants each year. The two most popular grants are the Pell Grant and the Federal Supplemental Educational Opportunity Grant (FSEOG). Both are awarded to undergraduate students in extreme financial need.

The Teacher Education Assistance for College and Higher Education (TEACH) Grant is available to college students who study to become teachers. To receive the grant, they promise to provide four years of teaching service after they graduate. If they fail to do so they must repay the grant money. Another way the Department of Education helps with financial aid is to offer resources for work-study positions. Students can earn money in jobs on campus that help pay for college.

The most basic financial aid offered by the Department of Education is student loans. Every student who wants to pursue further education after high school is able to take out student loans through the department. There are several different kinds of loans. Students can borrow enough to pay their expenses and start paying them back after graduation.

While student loans sound like an easy solution, there are complications. Students must pay interest on the loans. Interest is the cost of borrowing the money. It is charged by the month. The longer a student takes to repay a loan the more interest is owed. Loans plus interest can end up costing hundreds of thousands of dollars. And when students take out federal student loans, they are promising to repay the money. They must repay the loan no matter how long it takes.

George W. Bush visited a third-grade classroom in Chicago in 2008 in support of his No Child Left Behind Act.

There is a separate finance office that manages the Title I grants to states for low-income students based on how well the states prove their students have reached Common Core standards. States file paperwork showing how the grant money was used and also showing the improved results of assessment tests. The department can then decide how much money will be given to each state out of the lump sum it has to divide. Each state school district receives a basic funding level. Districts with a slightly higher number of poor students receive more funds on top of that. A more specific formula provides greater funding to high-poverty districts.

The Inspector General's Office: Education Crime Fighters

The Inspector General's office investigates crimes within the education industry. In one year the office nailed down guilty pleas in 21 cases of student aid fraud, six cases of stealing money from an elementary or high school, and six cases of stealing funds intended for public education programs. The office also brought down a conspiracy to defraud the post-9/11 GI Bill. Two women used veterans' names to get money for fake enrollment in online classes. Another college-level crime was committed by a university lecturer who sold fake health care program certificates.

One of the stranger cases the Inspector General's office pursued was about a man in Louisiana who falsified a FAFSA form. In fact, the man filled out the form with President Donald Trump's Social Security number, hoping to get private financial information about the president.

The Office for Civil Rights (OCR) follows up on complaints that violate federal laws against discrimination. Its particular focus is on discrimination in schools all the way from preschool to college. Complaints of discrimination and harassment in all of its forms are investigated by the Office for Civil Rights in partnership with the Department of Justice. Some of the antidiscrimination laws are older than the Education Department itself. For instance, Title IX, which forbids discrimination based on race, gender, or national origin, was passed in 1972. It was enforced by the Department of Health, Education, and Welfare until the creation of the Department of Education in 1979.

The Civil Rights office receives an average of 347 complaints of racial harassment each year. For instance, one complaint stated that several schools within the Lodi school district in California gave harsher punishments to black students than to white students even when the misdeeds were the same. The OCR investigated and found that Lodi had violated Title VI of the Civil Rights Act in numerous ways. As a result, the school district made improvements in the way it dealt with the student population.

Students with disabilities have also been subject to discrimination and harassment in schools. Investigators are called upon to look into complaints that students with behavioral disabilities are isolated or restrained in school settings. Many complaints say disabled students are not receiving free, appropriate public education.

Title IX is meant to ensure that female and male students have the same opportunities.

Enforcement of Title IX's ban on gender discrimination in all federally funded schools and programs is another responsibility of the OCR. Most gender discrimination complaints involve athletics. Although the inequality between men's and women's athletics has been greatly lessened since Title IX's enactment in 1972, total equality is still a long way off.

Title IX's athletics guidelines have a three-part approach. If any of these parts aren't achieved, it can be grounds for a complaint. Schools submit data to the OCR to show their compliance.

PART ONE: If the student body of a school is 60 percent male and 40 percent female, the amount of athletic opportunities must also be around 60/40. The proportions must match within a reasonable margin.

Since 2012 many complaints have been filed because colleges have eliminated men's athletic teams in sports such as golf, baseball, and fencing. They say the eliminations are to keep the schools Title IX-compliant, since the football teams have so many players but no women's sport equivalent. Eliminating other men's teams can satisfy the issue of proportion without trying to find team sports that would attract enough female players to satisfy the requirement and stay within budget.

PART TWO: The school must demonstrate a history and continuing practice of program expansion to ensure that both the male and female athletes are given equal opportunities and benefits.

This guideline includes providing comparable practice space, locker rooms, and coaching staff. Many complaints have been filed over the years about inadequate facilities for women's teams, or lack of transportation or training support such as men's teams receive. Some women's coaches who have complained to schools on their teams' behalf have been fired.

PART THREE: Schools must continue to make an effort to add activities that the underrepresented students are interested in, and to develop teams accordingly.

This is the hardest part of Title IX to track, since there is no data to report. When tracking a school's progress, the Office for Civil Rights often assumes that if they fail Part 2 they will probably fail Part 3.

Special Focus

The most high-profile cases that the OCR handles are complaints about sexual harassment and violence. They pursue complaints of discrimination or harassment based on:

- gender
- failure to conform to gender stereotypes
- actual or perceived sexual orientation

President Obama made the fight against sexual and domestic violence one of the cornerstones of his presidency. His administration's White House Task Force to Prevent Students from Sexual Assault created a resource guide to help students, schools, and communities deal with prevention, reporting, and investigation of crimes. Meanwhile, the Department of Education's Office for Civil Rights created new guidelines that K-12 schools and colleges or universities had to follow to collect information about any incidents. The new guidelines were far more time-sensitive and detailed than before. They led to a large number of new complaints being filed.

While the victims—mostly female—were relieved that their complaints were finally being treated seriously, many still felt wronged. The effort to provide greater protection and resolution for assault victims led to an outcry in favor of greater protection for those accused of committing the alleged assault. Many schools complained that the Title IX guidelines were too sensitive and ruined the lives of the accused student. Several colleges that had long histories of downplaying assault complaints were no longer able to avoid them. Accused students often avoided charges by transferring schools.

One example of the difficulties on campus is a case at the University of Notre Dame. In January 2016 a college football player allegedly sexually assaulted a female student. He smashed her phone when she tried to call for help and threatened her if she told anyone. Notre Dame's football players are campus celebrities, so she remained silent about the alleged assault until a few months later. Then another student claimed she was assaulted by the same person.

A complaint against the University of Notre Dame was filed in 2017 stating that a male student athlete was shown favoritism over the females he allegedly assaulted.

At that time the first woman he'd allegedly assaulted confided in a friend but still refused to report the assault to authorities, fearing revenge. Her friend reported it despite her fears. The school's Title IX office notified the female student that they would open an investigation. The process included identifying her to the football player, which is what she feared most. The Title IX officer suggested that if the student dropped the charges, they could close the case and the football player could transfer to a new school with a clean record. In 2017 the student filed a Title IX complaint against the university, saying the school had used its procedures to help the football player instead of his alleged victims.

In addition to cases of sexual assault, there are increasing complaints about bullying and harassment of students in the LGBTQ community (Lesbian, Gay, Bisexual, Transgender, Queer or Questioning). The most publicized issue is the restroom rule. Under the guidelines created by Obama, Title IX-protected students could use locker room and bathroom facilities that matched the gender with which they identify. However, in 2017 Trump withdrew federal guidance regarding locker room and restroom use. The decision about LGBTQ access is now decided state by state.

Obama's increased emphasis on combating student discrimination resulted in a monumental number of complaints. In 2016, his final year in office, the Office for Civil Rights received 16,720 complaints. With only 563 employees, almost the smallest staff in the department's history, they still managed to process 8,625 cases.

After Trump took office the focus on student discrimination lessened. The resource guides were no longer distributed. He had different ideas for the Department of Education.

As of 2017, states rather than the federal government can decide who is allowed to use gender-specific restrooms and locker rooms.

CHAPTER FIVE

Yesterday, Today, and Tomorrow

As the world has changed since the creation of the Elementary and Secondary Education Act, U.S. presidents have worked to advance the quality of the nation's education. They started with laws to provide federal funding to disadvantaged students, then laws to lessen discrimination. Amendments added over the years strengthened those goals. Presidents George W. Bush and Barack Obama spent 14 years collectively on educational reform that relied on standardized tests and shared curriculum goals. Whether the reforms were a success is still unclear. So, too, is the future direction of the Department of Education.

The idea of national education standards like the Common Core has taken a few hits. Some states didn't like the Common Core standards and didn't adopt them. They wrote their own standards instead. Others chose to keep key aspects of the Common Core and change the rest. The assessment tests were improved after the first few years. Still, many states chose to find alternative tests to use. The states each made their own choices about standards and curriculum.

Trump did not abolish the Department of Education when he took office. However, he made it clear that he thought it needed to operate differently. Trump promised to approach government as a business and that is how he looked at the department. His secretary of education, Betsy DeVos, brought in a plan to make education more businesslike. Her vision included more charter schools and school vouchers. Money was diverted from other programs in the Department of Education, many of which supported public schools and disadvantaged students. In the first budget submitted under the Trump administration, the Department of Education allocated $1.4 billion to fund scholarships, grants, and reward programs that would result in more charter schools. Many rules that had made it hard for charter schools to operate were changed too.

The educational policies implemented by past presidents are subject to change as each new administration takes office.

Charter schools and school vouchers are a touchy issue with many educators and public school districts because they affect school funding. Since charters are also public schools that are free to attend, funds follow students to the charter school if they switch. There are two kinds of charter schools. The original model of a charter school is one that was started by a group of teachers, parents, or other interested parties who made an agreement with the district. They operate the school as a nonprofit organization, meaning it isn't considered a moneymaking business. The funds they receive go back into running the school.

President Trump appointed Betsy DeVos education secretary in 2017.

The other kind of charter school is the for-profit model. A management company that operates charter schools gets the charter from the district and runs the school. The funds to run the school are paid to the management company. How those funds are used is up to the company. Many charter management operators have schools in districts all over the country, mostly in large cities with areas of low-performing schools. Teachers don't need any special qualifications, so management can save money on salaries by hiring untrained staff to teach. However, students must still pass the same state standardized tests as do students at every other public school. A 2017 Stanford University study showed that, although for-profit charter schools help students achieve the same standards in reading as public schools, math scores are much worse. Nonprofit charter schools post higher academic gains for their students than for-profit schools.

School vouchers also direct funds away from public schools. If a student is at a low-performing school and wishes to transfer to a better one, they can use a voucher to pay the fees at a different school. The voucher is like a check written by the government to offset the cost of private school tuition or public school fees. Vouchers are an especially popular idea with people who want to make private religious schools more affordable. The argument about the use of school vouchers dates back as far as 1954, when *Brown v. Board of Education* was passed. It was revived in the 1980s when Reagan wanted to give tuition tax credits to students wishing to attend private religious schools. Many people felt that using public funds to pay for religious education violated the Constitution's call for a separation between church and state. At the same time, many cases were being heard by the Supreme Court arguing in favor of tuition assistance. Finally in 2002 the Supreme Court ruled that vouchers could be used for religious schooling as long as nonreligious education choices were also available to the students.

At the 2017 March for Education in Washington, D.C., demonstrators called for federally funded support of public education.

The Little Department That Could

Changes have also been made to the way the Office for Civil Rights manages Title IX complaints. Obama had widened its reach to include many students who were socially vulnerable. He urged the office to open investigations into school districts if they suspected a pattern of harassment or ignoring student complaints.

Following Trump's directive to limit federal involvement in education, DeVos rolled back many protections in 2017. A program for survivors of campus sexual assault was eliminated, as was an anti-bullying initiative. Protections for children with disabilities and transgender students were also scaled back.

Higher education—colleges, universities, and career training—has also been affected by the change in administration. The Department of Education oversees accreditation, which means it confirms that institutions of higher learning maintain a certain level of quality. If a college or online university is accredited, its students can qualify for financial aid. If a school loses its accreditation or doesn't have it in the first place, the students may have heavy debts to pay and possibly no education to show for it.

One example, a company called Corinthian Colleges, ran dozens of career and technical colleges across the nation. In addition to government loans at a reasonable rate, students were offered financial aid in the form of high-interest loans through their colleges. Corinthian lured its students with promises of guaranteed job placement after graduation. Unfortunately, the education provided was inadequate and the job placement service didn't exist. Many students graduated unqualified for jobs in their chosen careers and with enormous student loan debt.

California Attorney General Kamala Harris announced the filing of a lawsuit against Corinthian Colleges in 2013.

In 2015 the Department of Education and the Consumer Fraud Protection Agency shut down Corinthian Colleges. Obama signed a bill that promised loan forgiveness for the defrauded students of Corinthian Colleges. The loan refunds would be managed through the Department of Education's Student Financial Aid office. Trump rolled back the bill in 2017. In December of that year DeVos announced that former students of Corinthian Colleges would have to repay a portion of their loans based on their current employment. The new ruling affected about 25,000 people.

As long as the Department of Education exists, its work will continue. Its small army of employees will ensure the grants and loans are processed, the data is crunched, and the information is shared. As long as the Office for Civil Rights exists, it will continue to uphold Title IX and investigate complaints in an effort to make educational institutions safe places for everyone.

Each president comes into office with new ideas about how to approach education. A president might choose to abolish the department. If that happens, its functions will be assigned to other areas of government. Dedicated members of the federal government will continue to support education with or without a department. State and local governments will remain committed to providing quality education. They know the future is in the nation's schools.

What would happen to your school if a president shut down the Department of Education?

Though some programs might be affected, schools receive most of their funding from state and local taxes. Many things would probably remain unchanged.

THE NACHOS ARE SAFE

The only government involvement in school lunches is by the United States Department of Agriculture, which oversees the nutrition guidelines in school menus. School districts pay for their own food service with some grant money from the USDA to help low-income students. Many schools in low-income districts also serve breakfast.

REV UP YOUR SEARCH ENGINE

Schools across the nation are adding tablets or laptops in the classroom. They are provided by grants from technology companies or district funds. That school-issued laptop connects students to online textbooks and student-friendly websites that are also chosen by the district.

LOOK AROUND

The school staff, including your teachers, the custodian who cleans up after your lunch hour, and the librarian who handed you this book are all hired and paid for by the school district.

What You Can Do

Someday you might want student financial aid. And someday you will be able to vote. Flex that muscle now! Google your state's U.S. senators and your district House representative. Their web pages should tell their official positions on education. Send them a letter or email them (better yet, both!) to say that you are a concerned student and future voter. Ask them to support continued education funding. Any time there is a news story about cuts or closures at the Department of Education, contact them again. Make your voice heard!

Timeline

1867

President Andrew Johnson creates the first Department of Education.

1957

President Dwight D. Eisenhower sends federal troops to Little Rock, Arkansas, to protect nine black students so they can attend a desegregated all-white high school for the first time.

1958

President Eisenhower authorizes the National Defense Education Act to subsidize science and engineering education after the launch of *Sputnik.*

1964

The Civil Rights Act is passed, forbidding discrimination based on race, nationality, color, or religion.

1965

The Elementary and Secondary Education Act is passed.

1972

Title IX is passed, forbidding discrimination based on sex.

1979

President Jimmy Carter creates the current Department of Education.

1983

The "Nation at Risk" report is published, saying American schools are failing.

1990

George H.W. Bush signs the American with Disabilities Act, a civil rights law that prohibits discrimination against people with disabilities in all areas of public life.

2002

George W. Bush launches No Child Left Behind education reform, which ties school performance to government funding.

2010

Common Core State Standards are put in place. States are encouraged to adopt the standards.

2017

President Donald Trump rolls back civil rights protections for transgender students and students with disabilities. He requests a $1.4 billion budget for charter school development.

Glossary

administrator—a person who manages

amendment—a change made to a law or legal document

appropriate—to set apart, authorize, or legislate for some specific use

boondoggle—a wasteful project, often involving dishonesty

compliance—in keeping with established rules and policies

conflict of interest—a conflict between the private interests and the official responsibilities of a person in a position of trust

dyslexia—a learning disability involving difficulties in reading, writing, and spelling

legacy—qualities and actions that one is remembered for; something that is passed on to future generations

legislation—the act of making laws

reform—to make or bring about social or political changes

segregation—separating people because of their skin color

Soviet Union—a Communist nation formed in 1922 when Russia combined with fourteen other republics in eastern Europe and central Asia; it broke apart in 1991

standard—something that is widely used or accepted as correct; in education, an achievement that demonstrates learning in a particular subject area

Additional Resources

Critical Thinking Questions

1. Do you think the government would have become involved in education even if the space race hadn't created the urgency for more scholars in the STEM fields? What other events might have prompted the nation to look more closely at its education system?
2. Should the federal government be involved in education? Should it be involved in setting standards? Should states be allowed to operate independently of the federal government and each other? Why or why not?
3. What are the benefits of charter schools and school vouchers in communities with low-performing public schools? Explain how they might improve student performance. What are some of the drawbacks of increasing the number of charter schools and voucher programs in the country?

Further Reading

Axon, Rachel. *Title IX Levels the Playing Field.* North Mankato, MN: Abdo Publishing, 2018.

Rissman, Rebecca. *Hidden Women: The African-American Mathematicians of NASA Who Helped America Win the Space Race.* North Mankato, MN: Capstone Press, 2018.

Rubin, Susan Goldman. *Brown v. Board of Education: A Fight for Simple Justice.* New York: Holiday House, 2016.

Walker, Paul Robert. *Remember Little Rock: The Time, The People, The Stories.* Washington, D.C.: National Geographic Children's Books, 2009 (reprinted 2015).

Internet Sites

Use Facthound to find Internet sites related to this book.

Visit www.facthound.com

Just type in 9780756559021 and go.

Source Notes

p. 10, "In contrast, Congress regularly approved ...." Education Department Budget History Table: FY 1980-FY2018 President's Budget. U.S. Department of Education, October 13, 2017. https://www2.ed.gov/about/overview/budget/history/index.html. Accessed on February 9, 2018.

p. 14, "President Eisenhower had to send ...." "Little Rock Nine." *Britannica Library*, Encyclopædia Britannica, January 2, 2018. ezproxy.naperville-lib.org:2606/levels/youngadults/article/Little-Rock-Nine/605810 Accessed on June 14, 2018.

p. 17, "He also authorized an official definition ...." Elementary and Secondary Education Act of 1965. *Social Welfare History Project* (2016). http://socialwelfare.library.vcu.edu/programs/education/elementary-and-secondary-education-act-of-1965 Accessed on January 6, 2018.

p. 23, "Their party platform states ...." S. 1141 — 102nd Congress: AMERICA 2000 Excellence in Education Act. www.GovTrack.us. 1991. https://www.govtrack.us/congress/bills/102/s1141 Accessed on June 16, 2018.

p. 24, "In addition, school districts receiving ...." "Development of the Elementary and Secondary Education Act." The Hunt Institute, http://www.hunt-institute.org August 2016. June 16, 2018. http://www.hunt-institute.org/wp-content/uploads/2016/09/Development-of-the-Elementary-and-Secondary-Education-Act-August-2016.pdf Accessed on June 16, 2018.

p. 24, "Congress, still controlled by Republicans ...." John W. Donohue "'Goals 2000: Educate America Act': notes for a chronicle." America, 18 June 1994, p. 6+. *General OneFile*, http://link.galegroup.com/apps/doc/ A15533748/GPS?u=napervillepl&sid=GPS&xid=ec14edb6. Accessed on June 16, 2018.

p. 31, "They created ...." Ashley Jochim, and Patrick McGuin. "The Politics of the Common Core Assessments." *Education Next*, Vol. 16, No. 4, Education Next Institute, Inc., 2016. Accessed on January 9, 2018.

p. 41, "The Civil Rights Office receives ...." "Report: Complaints to OCR Have Doubled Since 2005." *Campus Safety*, Clery/Title IX, https://www.campussafetymagazine.com/clery May 5, 2016. Accessed on June 19, 2018.

p. 51, "Non-profit charter schools post ...." *Charter Management Organizations* 2017. Center for Research on Education Outcomes, Stanford University, 2017. https://credo.stanford.edu. Accessed on February 14, 2018.

p. 51, "Finally in 2002 the Supreme Court ruled ...." "Shifting Boundaries: The Establishment Clause and Government Funding of Religious Schools and Other Faith-Based Organizations." *The Pew Forum on Religion & Public Life*. May 2009. Accessed on January 20, 2018.

p. 53, "Following Trump's directive ...." Clyde Wayne Crews Jr. "New Trump Executive Orders Spotlight Interior and Education Regulatory Dark Matter." *Forbes*, April 27, 2017. https://www.forbes.com/sites/waynecrews/ Accessed on June 19, 2018.

Select Bibliography

Alger, Vicki E. *Failure: The Federal Miseducation of America's Children.* Oakland, CA: Independent Institute, 2016.

Aspey, Susan, former assistant to Secretary Margaret Spellings at Department of Education (2006). Phone interview, October 18, 2017.

Baker, Bruce and Miron, Gary. "The Business of Charter Schooling: Understanding the Policies that Charter Operators Use for Financial Benefit." National Education Policy Center, School of Education, University of Colorado-Boulder, December 2015.

Dick, Steven J. "The Birth of NASA." NASA https://www.nasa.gov/exploration/whyweexplore/Why_We_29.html Accessed on October 16, 2017.

Frontline. "Are We There Yet?" Public Broadcasting System. http://www.pbs.org Accessed on October 16, 2017.

Howell, William. "Results of President Obama's Race to the Top." *Education Next*, Journal of Program on Education Policy and Governance, Harvard Kennedy School. Fall 2015. http://educationnext.org/results-president-obama-race-to-the-top-reform/ Accessed on October 16, 2017.

Jennings, Jack. *Presidents, Congress, and the Public Schools.* Cambridge, MA: Harvard Education Press, 2015.

McKay, Robert E. "LBJ the Teacher." *Humanities Texas*, July/August 2008.

National Center for Education Statistics. "Highlights from the 2000 Program for International Student Assessment (PISA)." https://nces.ed.gov/pubs2002/2002116.pdf Accessed on October 16, 2017.

Quick, Kimberly and Damante, Rebecca. "Louisville, Kentucky: A Reflection on School Integration." School Integration Report, Century Foundation, September 15, 2016. https://tcf.org/content/report/louisville-kentucky-reflection-school-integration/ Accessed on October 15, 2017.

Watters, Audrey. "How Sputnik Launched Ed-Tech." The History of the Future of Education Technology, Hack Education, June 20, 2015 http://hackeducation.com/2015/06/20/sputnik Accessed on October 15, 2017.

Index

About the Author

Amy Rechner is the author of more than 30 nonfiction books for children. She loves to do research and learn about new things and places. Amy lives in Chicago's western suburbs with her husband, daughter, and Nellie the Atomic Cat.